Written by Sam Conniff

Illustrations @ AdrianValencia
www.adrianvalencia.com

Design & Layout
by Elle Moss & Deanna Bains
www.drewlondon.co.uk

First published in 2021 by Sam Conniff Ltd

A catalogue record for this book is available from the British Library
ISBN 978-1-5272-9112-6

Set in Garamond Premier Pro Display

Printed in Great Britain by
Mixam, Watford, Herefordshire, WD25 7GS

With many thanks for your support to Sophia Thakur for poetry mentoring, Suzanne Hemming for self publishing mentoring, Bryony van der Merwe and Cindy Draughon for editing and Rye Books, for stocking a copy ready for Scarlett's birthday.

Unicorn Theory

By Sam Conniff & Scarlett Conniff Allende

For Scarlett,

Never let your imagination get squashed.
Thanks for teaching me how to play again.

Daddy. X

ACT 1

The Paradox of Pinky

Pinky is a little girl learning the hardest thing in life.

That sometimes the same thing can be wrong and still be right.

You see, a good thing can be bad and a bad thing can be good.

It's a very tricky truth that's often misunderstood.

Things now come in twos when they used to be one.

Two houses, two bedrooms, two toy sets to choose from.

Sounds too good to be true? Well it's way more cool:

Pinky gets double birthdays, but not double school!

YOU SEE, A GOOD AND A BAD THING

Unicorn Theory

THING CAN BE BAD
CAN BE GOOD.

13

There is a cost, of course, there is always a catch.

Pinky's parents seperated, they were no longer a match.

Life can be awesome with double sets on the shelf,

But life's not awesome when she feels doubled herself.

Sometimes two of her, sometimes more.

Which is the real one? Sometimes Pinky's not sure.

Some days seem like a game that she has to win,

it's a challenge to choose the right character to fit in.

Like all girls her age Pinky loves to play,

Making dens, making comics and messing about every day.

She loves her best friends, who love her right back,

But over her shoulder her little sister's keeping track.

Her parents expect her to remember a lot,

Teachers want her to enjoy what she does not.

She tries hard to be happy, and she is very funny,

Though try as she might, there's often worry in her tummy.

For a girl who just wants to have fun, she often feels blue.

For a girl still so young, she's got an awful lot to do.

ACT 2

Under the bed, into the universe

Pinky used to sleep well, but now spends the night waking;
she finds having two beds quite discombobulating.
Calling either parent brings them up on the double,
But waking her sister is a recipe for trouble.
Then late one night when the shadows came creeping,
Pinky tossed and turned, generally not sleeping.
She heard a whinny and snuffle from under the bed,
and leant over the side lowering her head.

Her bed was high enough for a slide but not big as a stable,

There squashed underneath was a beast from a fable.

Shining white, glowing pink and surprisingly glittery

Was a bright Unicorn; it made Pinky feel jittery!

"How do you do?" Pinky said ever so politely.

"I'm awesome," it said, smiling delightfully.

"I know your world's torn apart and it feels so confusing,

But it's just a new start, it needn't stay so bemusing."

Pinky asked, "Is it true there's a magic tattoo on your bum?"

"Of course," said the Unicorn,

"it's how we know what needs to be done.

Mine is a tear: I help children with sadness

I help them with fear and drive away badness."

"What do I need to do?" Pinky asked in return.

"You just need to believe and be ready to learn."

"Learn?" Pinky said, suddenly filled with suspicion.

The Unicorn smiled, "Learning's magic's nutrition!"

YOU JUST NEED

AND BE READY

TO BELIEVE
TO LEARN.

ACT 3

The midpoint of messiness and emotion

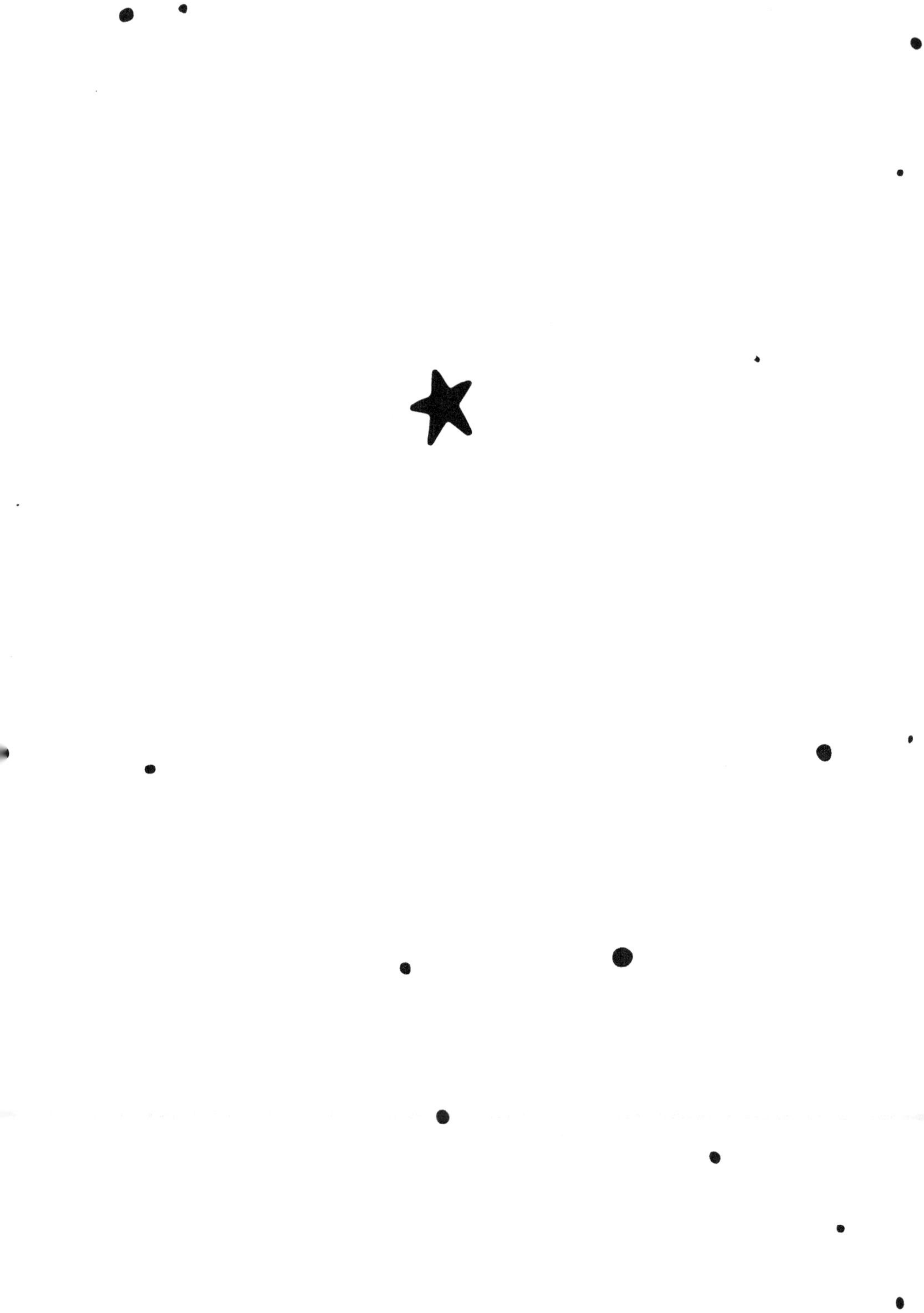

"Hop on! Grab my mane!" the Unicorn said.
"What's your name?" Pinky whispered once under the bed.
But when they fell through space where the floor once was
All she heard was the wind as they gatecrashed the cosmos.
They galloped down photons and leapt over stars,
And Pinky cheered when they danced around Mars.
"Where are we?" she asked as blood rushed to her head.
"The Universe," said the Unicorn, "the one under your bed."

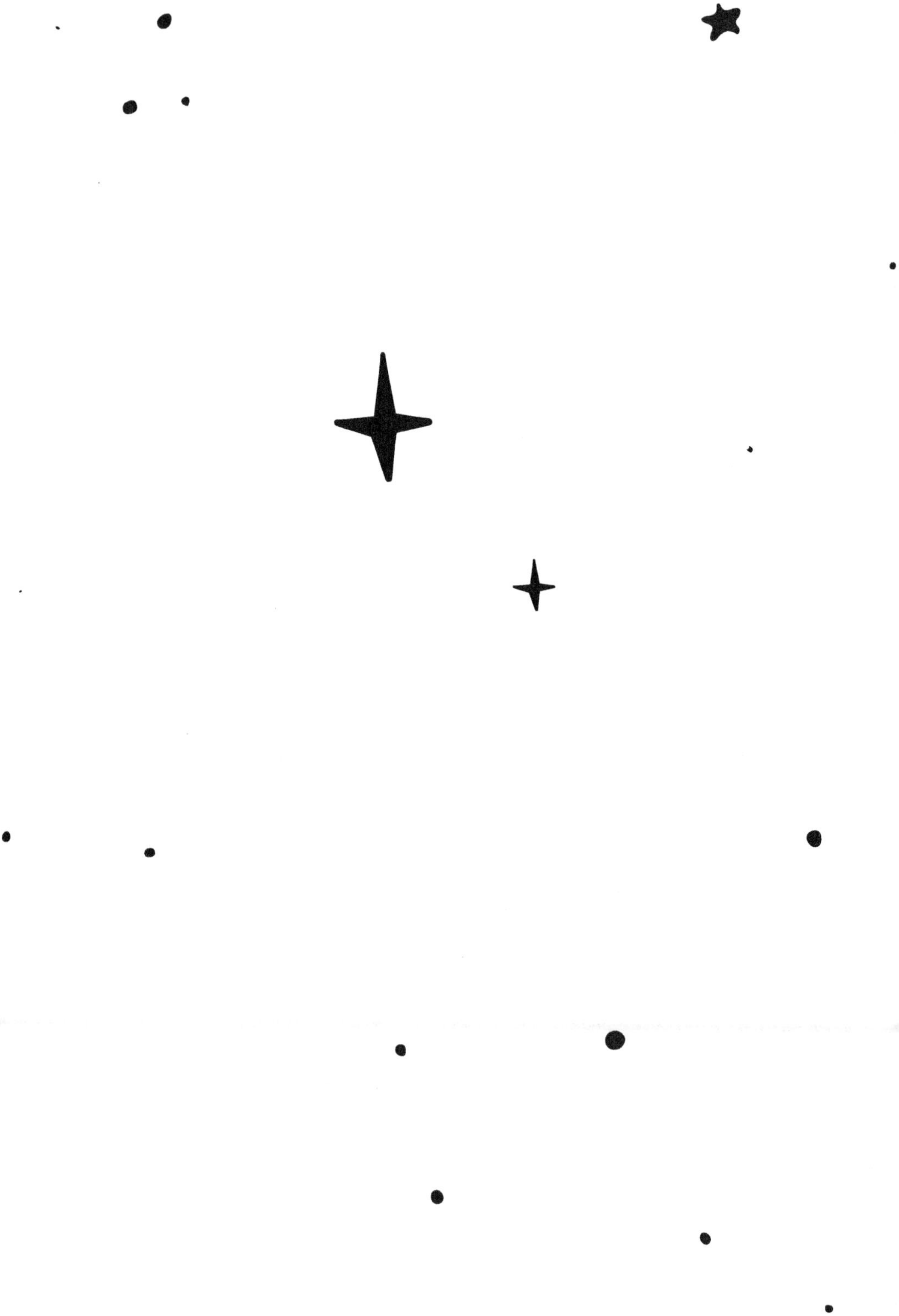

"I know you don't love science, the way it's taught in school,

But you are made from the same stuff as stars, and that's pretty cool.

They say Unicorns are magic, but really, that's gimmicks,

The secret of their power is just quantum physics!

Whether we're real or not comes from what you believe.

It's how wishes work. Life's what you conceive.

But things can get m e s s y

when

whole

things

d i v i d e,

Nothing stays the same, the trick is to enjoy the ride!"

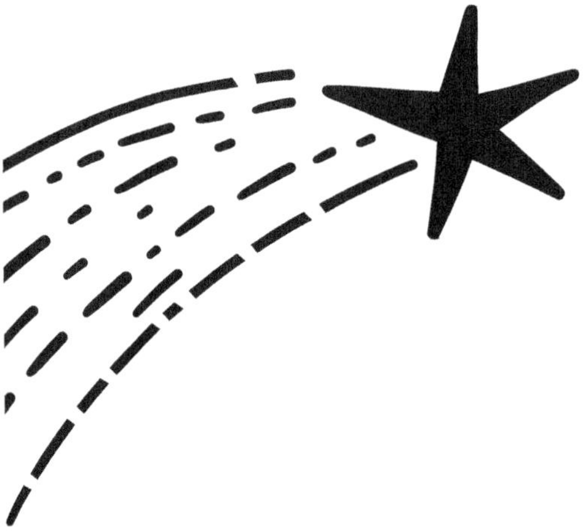

WHETHER
WE'RE NOT
WHAT YOU

WE'RE REAL OR
COMES FROM
BELIEVE.

Pinky's mind was racing, so much in her head.

Then all of a sudden, they were under a bed.

But it wasn't her room, another girl was in tears.

Pinky's heart felt her sobs, she could feel the girl's fears.

She climbed off the Unicorn, stepping into the room.

She took the girl's hand to get rid of the gloom.

"You'll be okay, because this sadness is healing.

You'll be okay, just as long as you keep feeling.

You'll be okay, because all nights become day.

You'll be okay, because tomorrow you'll play."

They left the girl feeling ten times stronger,

Pinky was left with ten times the wonder.

"But why didn't we use magic to fix her life better?"

"Well," said the Unicorn, "and now this gets meta...

Humans only truly grow when facing their fears,

When they're hugged by their bruises and caressed by their tears.

When they don't fear the future or the pain of the past,

When they can enjoy any moment, they learn and grow fast."

Flying back through space, stardust shone in her hair,

Pinky reflected on things she had learned out there.

"So, if the truth of everything, is everything will change,

Then why do I wish everything stays the same?"

"Your brain tries to protect you," the Unicorn explained.

"But you do have a choice. Your brain can be tamed.

Life is never what it seems at the very first glance,

And it's in opposites, and off-beats,

where we really learn to dance.

When things fall apart, of course everyone panics,

But messiness is natural, it's *the* second law of thermodynamics."

MESSINESS IS NATURAL,

IT'S THE SECOND LAW
OF THERMODYNAMICS.

For the rest of the year Pinky went out every night,

Riding her Unicorn, discovering magical sights.

The biggest lesson she learned is learning is play,

It became part of her life and she lives it each day.

She was happier now and found it so much fun

To help others switch their happiness back on.

When the friends parted, life still had ups and downs,

But Pinky had learned to make smiles out of frowns.

ACT 4

The crisis of conformity

Then one day when everything seemed so cool,
Pinky had to move to a brand new school.
Big school was boring, big school was no fun,
The lessons were endless, the teachers droned on.
Pinky knew that the secret of learning was play,
But teachers have a habit of getting in their own way.
Pinky protested, "Science is just play with intention."
And whilst she was right, she ended up in detention.

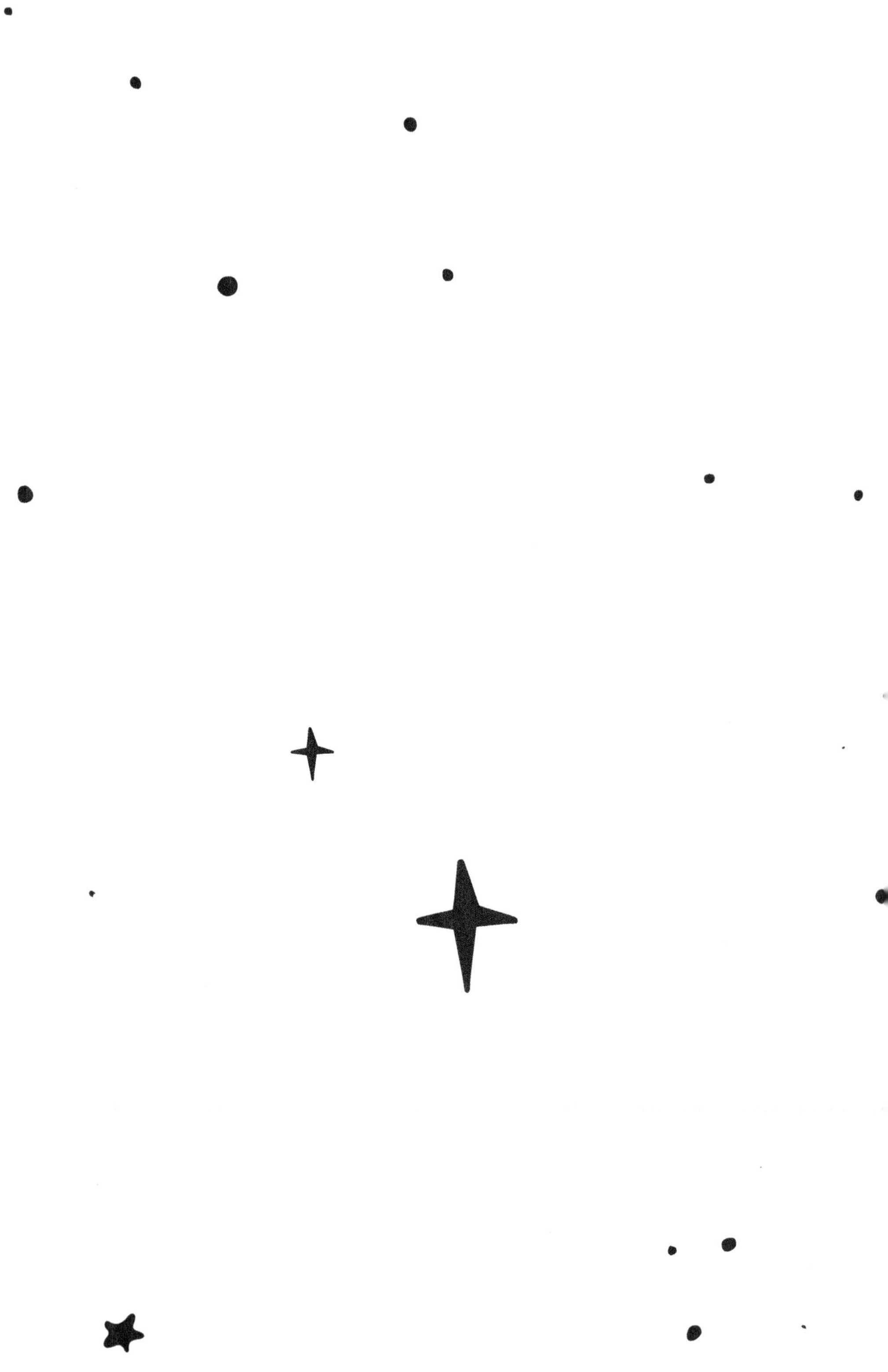

Having fun sucked out of school wasn't even the worst,
Suddenly everyone around her seemed to be cursed.
Where once play during playtime was always the aim,
Now everyone was focused on looking the same.
Fitting in, being mean and not standing out!
These things were weird things, Pinky wanted to shout.
But things always change, her friends fell in line,
And being different suddenly felt like a crime.

Again filled with sadness, Pinky lay in her bed.
I'm too old for Unicorns, she said in her head.
But she'd seen the universe and how it fits together,
She learned it's more important to explore than be clever.
Pinky saw getting old meant your imagination got squashed,
So she resisted growing up and getting brainwashed .
She called under the bed although it felt silly,
And felt the universe raise her hair, it's ever so chilly.
"You've grown," said her Unicorn ever so lightly.
"Time's flown," Pinky gasped, and hugged her so tightly

ACT 5

The ride home to resolution

Skidding past stars they flew on so excited,

Laughing at quasars, they were friends reunited.

"What happened?" said the Unicorn.

"I thought we learned sadness is a manageable illusion?"

"I grew up," Pinky said, "and that came with a fun transfusion."

The Unicorn laughed and Pinky did too,

The Unicorn winked and Pinky knew what she had to do.

The rest of the night was magic and play,

When Pinky got home, she was ready for the day.

SKIDDING PAST
STARS THEY FLEW
ON SO EXCITED,
LAUGHING AT
QUASARS, THEY WERE
FRIENDS REUNITED.

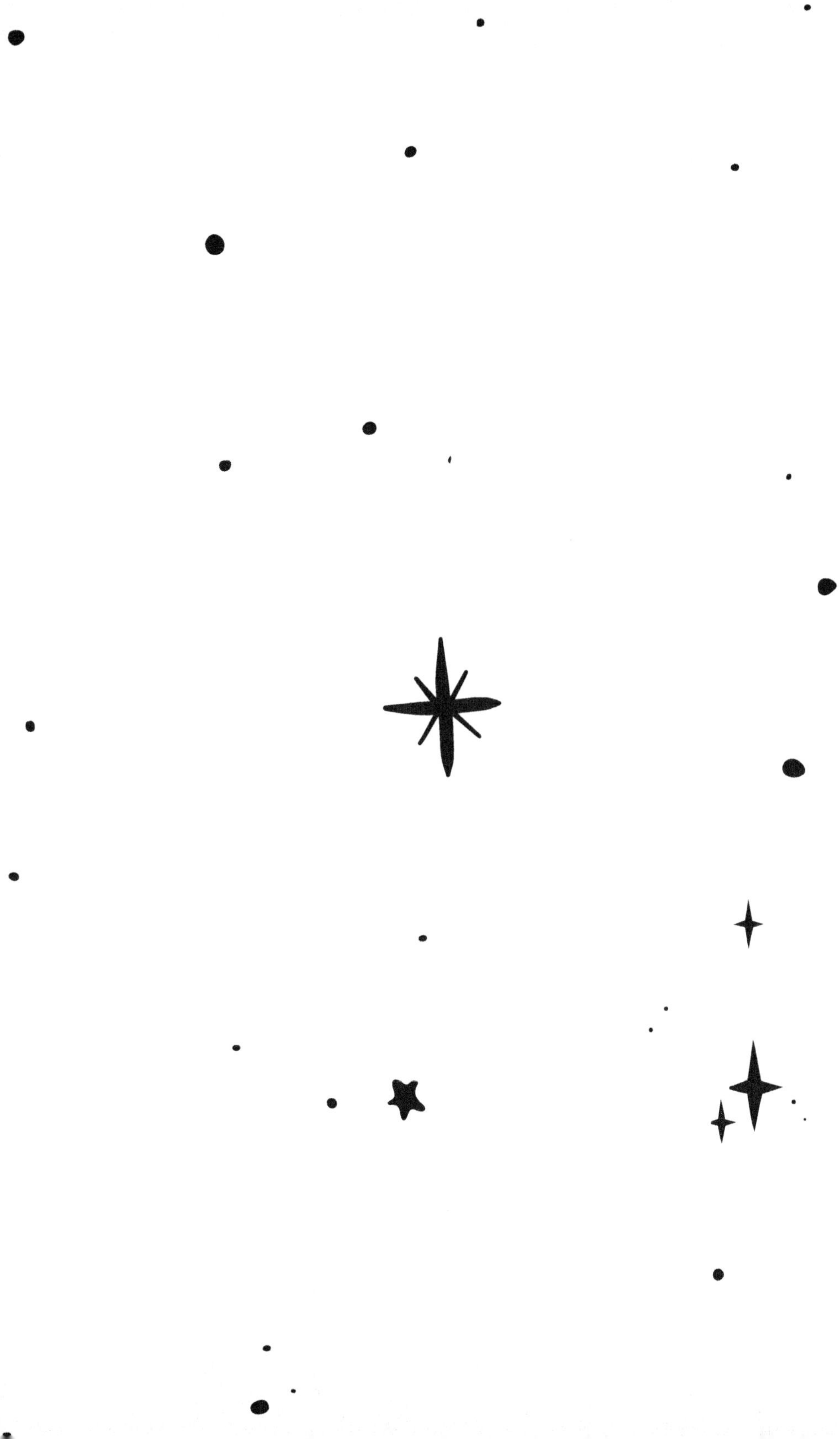

Life went on and most kids still fought to fit in,

But Pinky was strong, her new story well written.

She now knew life will always be changing,

And the way to prepare is to always keep playing.

To always explore, to always be on an adventure,

If she was always learning, nothing could quench her.

Most important of all, when life dealt her an unfair no,

Pinky learned to pretend that she'd actually heard **go!**

MOST IMPORTANT
OF ALL, WHEN
LIFE DEALT HER
AN UNFAIR NO,

PINKY LEARNED TO PRETEND THAT SHE'D ACTUALLY HEARD GO!

Pinky got older, but never forgot.

Growing up is a trap, but she wouldn't be caught

through school, and at uni, and at work while she earned

With her Unicorn beside her, she knew play let her learn.

When eventually one day she had kids of her own,

They too were lucky at night to be shown,

How to catch rides on a Unicorn at the end of each day,

And live life to its fullest, by never forgetting how to play.

THE END

(is just another beginning)

Printed in Great Britain
by Amazon

60426067R00041